W9-AQY-605

Easy Steps

to

GOOD GRAMMAR

A Mini-book for Self-Improvement

IDA R. BELLEGARDE

HARLO PRESS DETROIT, MICHIGAN

Other Books
By the Same Author

EASY STEPS
TO CORRECT SPEECH

LITTLE STEPPING STONES
TO CORRECT SPEECH

DEDICATION

To Dr. V. J. Coleman, whose encouragement and many suggestions inspired the publication of this book.

Second Printing, June 1973

Printed by
Harlo Press, 16721 Hamilton Avenue, Detroit, Michigan 48203

FOREWORD

This is not a comprehensive text on English grammar, but a small handbook to correct common faulty speech patterns. It is designed to take the fear out of grammar, to make learning correct grammar easy and pleasurable. There are no long-drawn-out rules to memorize, and no tests or quizzes. It has been designed to give the busy individual a ready-to-use working vocabulary that is grammatically correct in every way. Studied conscientiously, it can become a formula for instant grammar without embarrassment.

There is a good reason for the arrangement of this work. Common faulty expressions are listed above the corrected version, so that the reader may take a clear look at the offending phrases. There are no long-drawn-out explanations. Only the essentials are given. Exercises are then provided to correct each faulty speech habit separately. We have assembled only the necessary expressions. The material has been researched from the best educators in the field of speech, and combined into an easy-to-read book. Careful attention was given to the particular needs of the working individual and persons who are too busy to worry about the quality of their speech, yet who must speak well in order to be accepted.

The purpose of this book is to turn you into a flawless speaker with a minimum of time and effort. Daily drill will develop the habit of good grammar. Learning a few expressions every day will quickly turn you into a flawless speaker.

Through memorizing these ready-to-use expressions you will develop speech patterns that will last you throughout your lifetime. Your speech consists of many speech habits, and acquiring a habit means memorizing something that is learned so thoroughly that it becomes second nature. Repetition—that is suggested in this book—makes habit forming easy and pleasurable. It is easy to build a set of good speech habits by repeating the expressions so often that you begin to use them without being conscious of it, and without groping for words with which to express your ideas.

No longer will you have that uncomfortable feeling that you may be making mistakes of which you are not aware. For this book has covered the most commonly used expressions that you will need in your life. These expressions have been researched from the outstanding educators in the field of speech.

TABLE OF CONTENTS

THINGS TO REMEMBER

1. Some methods used in this book are not traditional, but the author's own, developed around the particular needs of her students.

2. Where there is more than one pronunciation for a word, we have used the preferred as listed in *Webster's New World Dictionary of the American Language,* published by The World Publishing Company.

3. All of the exercises must be done aloud.

4. This small book cannot, of course, include all of the ready-to-use expressions you will need. Use this book as a guide and work out the expressions you are in need of, using the ones in the book as models. To develop a large working vocabulary quickly, use a small notebook (3 x 5 inches) in which to record short statements and phrases. Take your notebook with you wherever you go and study in spare moments when you are not busy.

5. In the pronunciation key in parenthesis, double letters are used to indicate a long vowel or to emphasize the sound of a consonant. The syllable to be stressed is capitalized.

6. Good speech is a matter of practice. Drill. Drill. Drill.

1.

FAULTY SPEECH—I

Many speech defects are the result of imitation. We tend to speak as the people around us speak. This tendency to use neighborhood dialect may cause us to be considered illiterate. In this book you will have a series of exercises designed to correct these faulty speech patterns. *All of your exercises must be done aloud.* In every exercise you must learn the correct pronunciation of commonly mispronounced words as well as the correct grammatical expression. For our purpose in this book it is not necessary to remember *why* it is correct to use a certain expression. We are concerned with the correct use of the language, and not *why* it is correct. Below are two sets of expressions. The first expressions are *incorrect,* and all the second expressions are *correct.* Study the incorrect and correct expressions together until you are thoroughly conscious of the incorrect usage, then drill on the correct examples only.

Repeat the CORRECT examples ten times with each practice period putting more stress on the italicized words.

1. *Do not say: He don't* come often.
   Say instead: He doesn't come often.

2. *Do not say: She don't* care for him.
   Say instead: She doesn't care for him.
3. *Do not say: It don't* turn easy.
   Say instead: It doesn't turn easily.
4. *Do not say: Was you* there?
   Say instead: Were you there?
5. *Do not say: What kind of a* book is it?
   Say instead: What *kind of book* is it?
6. *Do not say: Was you* where you could hear?
   Say instead: Were you where you could hear?
7. *Do not say: Most* all the people believe him.
   Say instead: Almost all the people believe him.
8. *Do not say:* All the *peoples* are tired of taxes.
   Say instead: All of the *people* are tired of taxes.
9. *Do not say:* I am *sorta* tired.
   Say instead: I am *rather* tired.
10. *Do not say: Is you* going?
    Say instead: Are you going?

HE DON'T—CORRECTED

The habit of saying "He don't" "She don't" or "It don't" is a very bad one, but it can be broken easily by drilling on the following exercises until the correct expression becomes a part of your speech patterns. You can correct any faulty pattern you have developed by drilling on the correct way of expressing it. Repeat the following exercises aloud ten times with each study period, emphasizing the italicized words. Drill on each expression before going to the next.

1. *He doesn't* want to go without her.
2. *Doesn't he* know he can be fired?
3. She comes from the city, but *he doesn't.*
4. *He doesn't* know, but *he doesn't* know that *he doesn't* know.

5. *He doesn't* like children and pets, *does he?*
6. *He does not* want to go to school.
7. Where *does he* want to go, or *doesn't he* know?
8. *He doesn't* prepare his lesson well.
9. He feels that *he doesn't* deserve a better grade.
10. *He doesn't* care to be bothered.

SHE DON'T—CORRECTED

1. *She doesn't* like the weather, *does she?*
2. *Doesn't she* care for him anymore?
3. *She doesn't* like criticism.
4. *She doesn't* seem familiar with the subject.
5. *She does not* reach a conclusion.
6. *She doesn't* go anywhere.
7. *She doesn't* have a command of English
8. What *she doesn't* do is her own business.
9. Do her friends know *she doesn't* like to be teased?
10. *Does she,* or *doesn't she?* Only she knows for sure.

IT DON'T—CORRECTED

1. *It doesn't* seem logical.
2. You can be sure that *it doesn't* belong in here.
3. *Doesn't it* apply to animals as well as people?
4. Dignity is not one of his strongest points, but *it doesn't* seem to bother him.
5. Money is important but *it doesn't* buy happiness.
6. *It doesn't* matter about the weather, we shall go.
7. *It doesn't* look like rain.
8. No matter what *it does,* the puppy feels secure.
9. Knowing *it does* matter makes us feel better.
10. Buying the dress depends on whether *it does* or *it doesn't* fade easily.

IS YOU, WAS YOU—CORRECTED

Always use *are* and *were* with *you,* NEVER *is* or *was.* Repeat the following aloud ten times with each practice period, emphasizing the italicized words.

1. *Are you* going home today?
2. *Were you* at home yesterday?
3. *You are* perfectly capable of holding the job.
4. *Weren't you* aware of the impending storm?
5. *Aren't you* planning a vacation this summer?
6. *You are* facing a great opportunity.
7. *You weren't* convinced of his sincerity, were you?
8. *Are you* receiving your full share of happiness?
9. *Were you* intending to go tomorrow?
10. *You weren't* on time this morning.

MOST, ALMOST—CORRECTED

The two words "most" and "almost" will give you trouble if you are not conscious of their meanings. "Most" means the *greatest number* or the *greatest quantity.* "Almost" means *nearly.* Repeat the following aloud ten times with each practice period.

1. *Most* people like to read.
2. He possesses the *most talent.*
3. She won the *most votes.*
4. *Most exercise* is beneficial in some form.
5. *Most* of his *paintings* sold.
6. *Most* of the *rules* were broken.
7. *Most* of his *work* was wasted.
8. The *most* the room will seat is one hundred.
9. The day *most* people like is payday.
10. Mathematics is a subject *most* find to be difficult.

You may substitute *nearly* for *almost.*

1. *Almost every house* was painted white.
2. *Almost* the *entire congregation* contributed to the gift.
3. He paid *almost nothing* for his house.
4. He gave *almost twice* as many books as the church already had.
5. *Almost* the *entire choir* contracted colds.
6. *Almost every boy* had his hair cut.
7. She has *almost twice* as many dresses as her sister.
8. *Almost everyone* stayed away.
9. They were *almost* home when it started raining.
10. Have you *almost* finished reading the book?

2.

FAULTY SPEECH—II

Study the incorrect and correct expressions together until you are thoroughly conscious of the incorrect usage, then drill on the correct examples only. Repeat the CORRECT examples ten times with each practice period, putting more stress on the italicized words.

1. *Do not say: He have* come to the end of his row.
   Say instead: He has come to the end of his row.
2. *Do not say: They has* been kind to everybody.
   Say instead: They have been kind to everybody.
3. *Do not say: He blowed* his horn.
   Say instead: He blew his horn.
4. *Do not say: I have broke* my pencil.
   Say instead: I have broken my pencil.
5. *Do not say: He brang* it to me yesterday.
   Say instead: He brought it to me yesterday.

6. *Do not say: He had brung* it last week.
   Say instead: He had brought it last week.
7. *Do not say: He come* over yesterday.
   Say instead: He came over yesterday.
8. *Do not say: Has* he *came* yet?
   Say instead: Has he *come* yet?
9. *Do not say: He begun* to tell the story.
   Say instead: He began to tell the story.
10. *Do not say: He busted* his balloon.
    Say instead: He burst his balloon.

HE HAVE, SHE HAVE, IT HAVE, THEY HAS—CORRECTED

The habit of saying "he have" "they has" "she have" and "it have" is almost an unforgivable sin. You can correct this faulty pattern of speech by drilling on the following exercises until they become firmly embedded in your working vocabulary. Repeat the following aloud ten times with each study period, emphasizing the italicized words. All of the following are correct.

Say: He has

1. *He has* prepared the food.
2. *He has* confused the enemy.
3. *He has* a famous relative.
4. *He has* withdrawn his claim.
5. *He has* forsaken his country.
6. *Has he* gone home?
7. *Has he* designed the suit?
8. *Has he* moved yet?
9. *Has he* been discouraged before?
10. *Has he* applied himself well?

Say: She has

1. *She has* had her fortieth birthday.
2. *She has* a graceful figure.
3. *She has* used her office for personal gain.
4. *She has* put her foot down.
5. *She has* played the fool.
6. *Has she* succeeded?
7. *Has she* a serious attitude?
8. *Has she* become involved in work?
9. *Has she* been inspired?
10. *Has she* been amused by the incident?

Say: It has

1. *It has* been ten years.
2. *It has* become a national symbol.
3. *It has* a fragile structure.
4. *It has* a familiar ring.
5. *It has* united the two of them.
6. *Has it* been that long?
7. *Has it* affected their relationship?
8. *Has it* touched a responsive chord?
9. *Has it* covered the important points?
10. *Has it* functioned well?

Say: They have

1. *They have* met the enemy.
2. *They have* been tactless and brash.
3. *They have* obtained ownership.
4. *They have* learned to adjust.
5. *They have* known each other for ten years.
6. *Have they* been invited?

7. *Have they* built for the future?
8. *Have they* failed to examine the facts?
9. *Have they* expressed their desires?
10. *Have they* been feuding lately?

3.

FAULTY SPEECH—III

THE PRONOUN "I"

You must be careful in using the pronoun "I." The statement, "Aren't I?" is incorrect and should never be used. "Am I not?" is the correct expression in this case. Practice the following exercise until you automatically use the correct expressions.

1. *Do not say: I has* prepared my lesson.
   Say instead: I have prepared my lesson.
2. *Do not say: I stops* each afternoon for a rest.
   Say instead: I stop each afternoon for a rest.
3. *Do not say: I works* very hard at improving myself.
   Say instead: I work very hard at improving myself.
4. *Do not say: I reads* until bedtime.
   Say instead: I read until bedtime.
5. *Do not say: I sings* when I work.
   Say instead: I sing when I work
6. *Do not say: I hasn't* seen his new car.
   Say instead: I haven't seen his new car.
7. *Do not say: I laughs* at people who are lazy.
   Say instead: I laugh at people who are lazy.
8. *Do not say: I walks* every day for exercise.
   Say instead: I walk every day for exercise.
9. *Do not say:* I am smart, *aren't I?*
   Say instead: I am smart, *am I not?*

10. *Do not say: I works* a puzzle each day.
    Say instead: I work a puzzle each day.

4.

NOUNS, PRONOUNS, AND VERBS

Nouns are the names of things or people, such as, *town, house,* or *Mary.* When a noun means only one thing it is said to be singular, such as *house* and *John.* When a noun means more than one thing it is said to be plural, as *houses, boys,* or *girls.* Nouns usually form their plurals by adding *s* or *es.* There are exceptions to this rule but we will not talk about them here.

Pronouns are words used instead of nouns, such as, *it* for *town, she* for *Mary, he* for *John,* or *they* for *girls.* Therefore, a pronoun is a word used to indicate something or someone without using the name. *You, it, they, him, we, your, whose, this,* and *whoever* are all pronouns. When a verb is placed *before* a pronoun, the pronoun becomes an *object* and therefore must change to the *objective* form. (Note: There is an exception to this rule: *When any form of the verb BE is used, the pronoun following it must be in the subjective form.* Forms of the verb *be* are: *am, is, was, are,* and *were.* This exception will be studied later.)

Below are examples of *object pronouns* following *verbs.*

1. She *sent me* an invitation.
2. He *gave us* time to eat.
3. We *taught him* a lesson.
4. He *followed her* home.
5. He *talked them* into stayng.

Verbs are words that express action or being. The most common verbs are action words, such as *think, do, go, sit, stand, come, know* and *eat.* Verbs are also singular or plural. But unlike nouns they usually form their plurals by DROPPING the *s* or *es.* Always remember that (usually) *adding s or es to a verb makes it singular; adding s or es to a noun makes it plural.*

A verb is a word used with nouns or pronouns to tell something about them. A verb tells what is, what is done, or what is being done. When a verb is used with a plural noun, it also must be plural; when it is used with a singular noun it must be singular.

Repeat each statement ten times at each practice period. Be sure to put more stress on the italicized words. Emphasize the final *s's* in the singular forms.

The first line shows correct usage of *verbs with subject nouns;* the second line shows correct usage of *verbs with pronouns.*

1. *John sings* while *he works.*
   He sings while he works.
2. *Mona is* a good girl.
   She is a good girl.
3. The *bell has* a loud ring.
   It has a loud ring.
4. *Dorothy plays* the piano well.
   She plays the piano well.
5. *Joseph does* a good job.
   He does a good job.
6. *Mary and Sue sing* beautifully.
   They sing beautifully.
7. *Mona and Mary are* well-behaved girls.
   They are well-behaved girls.
8. The *bells have* been broken.
   They have been broken.

9. *Dorothy and Sue play* the piano well.
   They play the piano well.
10. *Joseph and John do* a good job.
    The *boys do* a good job.

5.

TROUBLESOME NOUNS

Some nouns that may give you trouble are the few that have the same form for both singular and plural. Some of them are: *deer, sheep, salmon, swine, trout, gross* and *vermin.* Learn how to use these nouns by drilling on the following exercise. Remember you must never add *s* on these nouns to form a plural.

1. *One deer* grazed in the pasture.
2. *Five deer* stared across the fence.
3. *One sheep* remained in the field.
4. The farmer led *three sheep* to market.
5. *A salmon* spawns in the spring.
6. Mother baked five *salmon* in the oven.
7. *One* little *swine* is called a pig.
8. *Five* big *swine* are called hogs.
9. I caught *one trout* from the brook.
10. Yesterday I caught *five trout.*
11. *A gross* of pencils will be needed.
12. *Ten gross* of pencils were shipped.
13. *A vermin* is a disgusting animal.
14. *These vermin* must be controlled.

Another group of nouns that may give you trouble are the ones that are plural in form but singular in meaning. These nouns end in *s* but are really singular. Some of these are: *mathematics, news,* and *physics.* Repeat the following ten times, emphasizing the italicized words.

1. *Mathematics is* considered a difficult subject.
2. *Mathematics was* taught in the lower grades.
3. *Mathematics has* always been taught in schools.
4. Good *news seems* to be rare these days.
5. Local *news is* reported every hour.
6. The *news* of his promotion *was* reported today.
7. *Physics is* an important science in the space age.
8. *Physics has been* expanded through experimentation.

Some nouns that end in *s* may be used in both the singular and the plural. Some of them are: *athletics, politics, ethics,* and *statistics.* Repeat the following aloud ten times, emphasizing the italicized words.

1. *Athletics has* become an important part of college life.
2. *Athletics have* dominated our national field of recreation.
3. *Politics are* practiced by many well-meaning politicians.
4. *Politics is* sometimes considered a national sport.
5. *Ethics is* a subject that should be taken seriously.
6. *Ethics were* involved in solving the case.
7. *Statistics is* necesssary in the running of good government.
8. *Statistics were* important in arriving at an equitable settlement.

Some nouns ending in *s* or *es* are always plural in form and meaning. Some of these are: *scissors, annals, ashes, billiards, drugs, goods, proceeds, suds, riches, tidings, tongs, trousers, vitals, thanks* and *alms.* Repeat the exercise aloud ten times, emphasizing the italicized words.

1. The *scissors are in* the basket.
2. The *scissors have been* sharpened.

3. The historical *annals were* sent out today.
4. The *ashes were* blown out to sea.
5. Illegal *drugs were* sold over the counter.
6. *Goods have* been shipped to the buyer.
7. *Proceeds* from the rally *were* given to the priest.
8. *Suds are* good to clean the rug.
9. *Riches are* sometimes a hindrance.
10. The *tongs were* hanging on the wall.
11. His *trousers were* torn.
12. Polite *thanks were* sent.
13. *Billiards are* considered fun to play.
14. *Alms were* donated for the poor.

Other nouns that may give you trouble are those that have different spellings for the plural form. They form their plurals by means other than adding *s* or *es.* The most common are: *man, woman, child, ox, goose, mouse, foot, louse, tooth,* and *titmouse* (a species of small bird). Remember, you will be called illiterate if you add *s* on *man, woman,* or *child* to form the plural. Drill on the following exercise until you are sure.

1. *One ox was* used to pull the plow.
   Five oxen were used to pull the wagon.
2. *The child* came in crying.
   Children play in the meadow.
3. His *foot was* hurt.
   His *feet were* hurt.
4. *A mouse is* a small rodent.
   Mice are small rodents.
5. *A* snow *goose* swam on the lake.
   Snow *geese fly* south in the winter.
6. The *man walked* away from the wreck.
   Five men were hurt in the wreck.

7. He had *a tooth* pulled.
   He had *three teeth* pulled.

Some less common nouns that have different spellings for the plural form are listed in the exercise below. Repeat ten times, emphasizing the italicized words. Study the pronunciation carefully.

1. *One alumnus* (a LUM nus, masculine singular) said that he would go.

2. *Two alumni* (a LUM ni, masculine plural) said that they would go.

3. *One alumna* (a LUM na, feminine singular) tore her dress at the party.

4. *Five alumnae* (a LUM nee, feminine plural) sang at the party.

5. He made *an analysis* (a NAL i sis) of the article.

6. He made *five analysis* (a NAL i seez) of the books he had read.

7. *A parenthesis* (pa REN the sis) is made of two curved lines.

8. The author used *three parentheses* (pa REN the seez) to explain the material.

9. *One bacterium* (bak TEER i um) was isolated under the microscope.

10. *Thosuands* of *bacteria* (bak TEER i a) were found in the polluted water.

11. He based his conclusions on *one criterion.* (kri TER i on)

12. He used *fifty criteria* (kri TEER i a) upon which to form a judgment.

13. Write a *synopsis* (si NOP sis) of the story.

14. Write *synopses* (si NOP seez) of three of your favorite books.

Note: The pronunciation key used in this book is usually the author's own, developed around the needs of her students.

TROUBLESOME COMPOUND NOUNS

When compounded nouns are written with a *hyphen,* the main word in the group is made plural.

1. Her sister-in-law won a cooking contest.
2. Her three *sisters-in-law* came to the reception.
3. The man-of-war steamed out to sea.
4. The navy launched three *men-of-war* within a period of three months.

When a compound noun is written *without* a hyphen the *ending* is made plural.

1. The airship returned safely to its base.
2. Many *airships* flew daily over the war zone.
3. His birthday fell on Friday, but his parents' *birthdays* came on Sunday.
4. *One cupful* of sugar is enough.
5. It takes *five cupfuls* of water to fill the bowl.
6. Put *one spoonful* of soda in a glass of milk.
7. *Three spoonfuls* of soda will be too much in the gingerbread.

PRECEDED BY A NUMBER

The plural of certain words that denote quantity or measure of weight is formed by adding *s* to the singular, except when the words are preceded by a number. Study the following carefully.

1. *Dozens* of roses were sent to the celebrity.
2. The ship weighed *hundreds* of tons.
3. *Thousands* of men were recruited for the army.

4. *Millions* of dollars are spent foolishly.

The following nouns are preceded by a number:

1. *Two dozen* roses were given to the singer.
2. The ship weighed *seven hundred* tons.
3. *Ten thousand* men were recruited for the army.
4. He lost *three million* dollars on the deal.

6.

THE COMPOUND SUBJECT

The compound subject in which two or more words are joined by *and,* and used as the subject will give you trouble if you do not study them carefully. Most compound subjects must take a plural verb. Study the following sentences.

1. John and Henry *were* at the show.
2. Horses and mules *are* used as draft animals.
3. Her husband and her son *were* worried about her health.
4. The textbook, notebook, and pencil are all you need.
5. The rose, the jasmine, and the violet *smell* equally as sweet.

AN EXCEPTION

At times a compound subject may take *either* a singular or a plural verb. It depends on the meaning intended. If the two or more words in the subject constitute *one* idea, the subject takes a *singular* verb. Study the sentences below.

1. Bread and butter *is* good for children. (Bread and butter is considered one food).
2. My sister and confidante *is* coming to visit us. (One person).
3. My brother and man Friday *is* always beside me. (One person).

ANOTHER EXCEPTION

If the words are joined by *and* are preceded by such words as *each, every, many a,* or *no* a singular verb is always required. Study carefully the following sentences.

1. Every man, every woman, and every child *was* standing at attention when the flag was unfurled.

2. Each student and each teacher *hopes* to have an early vacation.

3. No talking and no gum-chewing *is* permitted in church.

4. Many a pet and many a child *has* been refused admittance to the rooming house.

COMPOUND SUBJECTS JOINED BY ALTERNATIVE WORDS

There are compound subjects joined by alternative words, (words indicating a choice between two things) such as *either—or, neither—nor,* and *not only—but also.* When words of a compound subject are joined by alternative words, the verb is *singular* IF the subject words are *singular,* but *plural* if the subject words are *plural.* Study the following sentences. Remember that *neither* goes with *nor, either* with *or,* and *not only* with *but also.*

SINGULAR SUBJECT WORDS

1. Either Ruth or Rita *is* going.

2. Either the father or the son *was* driving the car.

3. Neither the boy nor the girl *is* here.

4. Not only your speech, but also your appearance *is* important.

PLURAL SUBJECT WORDS

1. Either roses or gardenias *are* needed for the wedding.
2. Either the girls or the boys *are* guilty.
3. Neither the instructors nor the students *were* prepared for the test.
4. Not only the boys but also the girls *were* there.

IMPORTANT EXCEPTIONS

However, if the subject parts differ in number, the verb agrees with the noun nearest to it. Study the following.

1. Either the sons or their *father is* going.
2. Either the father or his *sons are* going.
3. Neither the students nor the *teacher was* there.
4. Neither the teacher nor the *students were* there.
5. Either the dog or the *children are* responsible for overturning the box.

Either the children or the *dog is* responsible for overturning the box.

7. Not only the mother but also the *children were* frightened.
8. Not only the children, but also the *mother was* frightened.

7.

COLLECTIVE NOUN USED AS SUBJECT

A collective noun is a word which denotes a collection of individuals or things thought of as a whole as, flock and army. A collective noun is usually singular in form and as such takes a singular verb. Study the following.

1. The *jury is* deliberating.
2. It is said that the *army marches* on its stomach.

3. The Apache *tribe was* the last to surrender to the U.S. Army.
4. The history *class is* always the last to give in on an argument.
5. The *club is* going on a picnic.
6. The *committee is* not meeting this evening.
7. A *flock* of quail *is* wandering through the grass.
8. A *herd* of deer *is* grazing in the meadow.

AN EXCEPTION

A collective noun may take a *plural* verb when the in-individuals of the group are thought of *separately*. Usually, it makes little difference whether you use a singular or a plural verb. Below are examples of a collective noun taking a plural verb.

1. The *club are* not agreed on a place for the picnic.
2. The *family were* happy to be back home.
3. This *class are* planning their summer vacations.

8.

INDEFINITE PRONOUNS

Indefinite pronouns are pronouns that do not refer to any specific person or thing. Most of the indefinite pronouns are singular, such as, *either, neither, each, another* and *one.* Study the following.

1. *Either is* qualified to speak.
2. *Either is* capable of completing the job.
3. *Either is* good enough.
4. *Neither is* going today.
5. *Neither was* there when it happened.
6. *Neither is* working at this time.

7. *Each is* his own protector.
8. *Each was* graciously received.
9. *Each was* pleasantly impressed.
10. *Another is* likely to follow.
11. We decided that *another was* too many.
12. *One is* not capable of making decisions under those conditions.
13. *One makes* more friends by being oneself than by putting on airs.

ONE, BODY, AND THING

All compounds of one, body, and thing are singular. Repeat the following sentences until you can use these words correctly without thinking. Emphasize the italicized words.

1. *Everyone is* going.
2. *No one was* surprised.
3. *Anyone is* able to do it.
4. *Someone is* sure to complain.
5. *Anybody is* welcome to it.
6. *Is anyone* home?
7. *Nobody wants* to be found guilty.
8. *Everybody was* asked to contribute.
9. *Anything is* likely to happen.
10. *Nothing is* for certain.
11. *Everything was* whirling around.
12. *Something is* going to happen.
13. *Somebody was* calling the dog.
14. *Nobody was* willing to go.

Note: The indefinite pronoun *both* is plural. The indefinite pronouns: *all, any, some, none,* and *such* are used both in the singular and in the plural.

9.

THE LY CONFUSION

Most words used with an action word (verb) end in ly, but all such words do not end in *ly*. This is a source of confusion for some people. The action words are verbs and the words used with them are called adverbs. Some adverbs have two forms, one with the *ly,* and one without the *ly*. It is easy to remember, when not to use the ly: when giving a command, making a request, or giving instructions do not use the *ly*. The most common adverbs, however, end in *ly*. Memorize the following by frequent repetition.

ADVERBS ENDING IN LY

1. She *walked bravely* through the dark and gloomy forest.
2. He *walked sadly* from the room.
3. He *stared coldly* at the opposing team.
4. She *spoke softly* and *quietly* to the frightened children.
5. She *rose quickly* from her chair.
6. He *felt deeply* the loss of a friend.
7. He *thought highly* of the men with whom he worked.
8. She *came quickly* from the house.
9. He *drove slowly* along the road.
10. The frightened children *held tightly* to each other.
11. He *tied* the string *loosely* around the package.
12. She *plays* the piano *beautifully.*
13. She *smiled sweetly* across the room.
14. The sun *shone brightly* through the trees.
15. The sun *sank slowly* below the horizon.
16. He *worked* the puzzle *easily.*

ADVERBS WITHOUT LY

When giving a command, making a request, or giving instructions DO NOT use *ly.* Drill on the following statements until you have them firmly established in your mind.

1. You must *play fair* with the boys.
2. *Drive slow* when crossing the bridge.
3. *Come quick!* The pot is boiling over.
4. *Aim high* in life and you'll succeed.
5. *Cast* the net *wide,* and hold the rope tight.
6. *Open* your mouth *wide.*
7. *Breathe deep* and hold your breath.
8. *Hold tight* to each other when crossing the road.
9. He *runs fast* on the practice field.
10. *Strike* the ball *hard.*

TROUBLEMAKERS

Not all words following action words (verbs) are adverbs. Some are descriptive words, called adjectives and do not end in *ly.* It is easy to recognize these troublemakers. If the action word can be replaced by *is, are, was,* or *were,* the word following it is an adjective and should NOT end in *ly.*

Memorize the following by frequent repetition.

1. The table *feels smooth* to the touch.
   The table *is smoot*h to the touch.
2. The roses *smell sweet.*
   The roses *are sweet.*
3. The bell *sounded* too *loud.*
   The bell *was* too *loud.*
4. The medicine *tasted bitter.*
   The medicine *was bitter.*
5. She *looked beautiful* in pink.
   She *was beautiful* in pink.

6. The hole *looked deep.*
   The hole *was deep.*
7. The puzzle *appeared easy.*
   The puzzle *was easy.*
8. Her voice *sounded soft.*
   Her voice *was soft.*
9. He *felt sad.*
   He *was sad.*
10. She *looked brave.*
    She *was brave.*

10.

WHO AND WHOM

The pronouns *who* and *whom* will be considered separately because of the difficulty they present to the majority of persons. All the rules applied to pronouns are applied to *who* and *whom.* Who is the *subject* form and whom is the *object* form. Memorize the following sentences, and use them as models to work out your own expressions.

The Subject *Who*

1. *Who* shall I say is calling?
2. She was a woman *who* he thought could do the work.
3. Do you know *who* was selected?
4. *Who* did he say called?
5. He is the man *who* you thought was her father.
6. *Who* do you think did it?
7. *Who* is he, do you suppose?

The Object *Whom*

1. *Whom* did you call?
2. Of *whom* are you speaking?
3. With *whom* did you talk?

4. To *whom* did you send the money?
5. *Whom* shall we invite to the party?
6. *Whom* shall I give it to?
7. For *whom* will you vote?

11.

WHOEVER AND WHOMEVER

The Subject *Whoever*

1. Give the prize to *whoever* deserves it.
2. *Whoever* did it should be proud.
3. Give the money to *whoever* needs it most.
4. It is for *whoever* merits it.
5. Invite *whoever* you think will come.
6. I want to work with *whoever* is prepared.

The Object *Whomever*

1. Tell it to *whomever* you like.
2. She smiled at *whomever* she met.
3. You may invite *whomever* you choose.
4. The book is for *whomever* you select.
5. Give the flowers to *whomever* you meet.
6. He imprisoned *whomever* he disliked.

12.

FAULTY SPEECH—IV

One of the most common speech faults is that of telescoping words, that is, running words together. Everyone is guilty of this fault at times, but careful speakers try not to let it become a habit. The most common expressions are the ones shown below. Practice the correct expressions by repeating each five times with each practice period, being careful to pronounce the words clearly and distinctly.

Do Not Say:	*Say Instead:*
1. can'cha	can't you
2. cood'ya	could you
3. dya	do you
4. glad to mee cha	glad to meet you
5. gun'na or gon'na	going to
6. god'da	got to
7. has'ta	has to
8. haf'ta	have to
9. let'ta	let her
10. let-em	let him
11. lem'me	let me
12. odd'a	ought to

13.

CONCERNING RULES

It is not necessary to know all the rules of grammar to speak correctly. If you will consciously memorize certain basic speech patterns, expressions that the best speakers use, you can speak perfect English without knowing the rules that govern good speech. We are not saying that this is the better way. We are only saying that it is highly possible, and can be done easily. All you need is a little determination.

However, there are times when we must revert to reviewing some rules in order to present the material more clearly. This is one of those times. We must discuss some rules governing verbs, that is, words of action.

14.

ACTION WORDS ENDING IN ED

When final *ed* represents past time of a verb, (without forming an extra syllable) it is pronounced *d* IF the sound before it is a *voiced* sound. But if the sound before it is a whispered sound, the *ed* is pronounced like t. *For* example, begged is pronounced (begd), but *baked* is pronounced (bakt).

In speaking, there are two kinds of sounds: voiced sounds, and voiceless or whispered sounds. Voiced sounds, are made with a murmur or hum. Voiceless sounds are whispered; you do not use the voice.

THE SOUND OF K

K is a whispered sound. It is made by pressing the back of the tongue against the hard palate, while building up the breath, then forcing the tongue away suddenly and forcefully *without making a sound with your voice.*

Practice the K sound by pronouncing the following words. Exaggerate the K sound.

walk, talk, ask, bake, look, luck, milk, rake, work.

Note: Do not pronounce the *L* in walk and talk.

15.

I AXED HIM

One of the saddest errors made in English speech is the mispronunciation of the three-letter word *ask.* Many people are not aware that this speech fault may brand them as being illiterate and ignorant. You must never pronounce *ask* as *ax* or *axe.* An *axe* (pronounced, aks) is a tool for chopping trees

or splitting wood. *Ask* (pronounced, azk) means to make a request. To clear up this bad speech fault repeat the following aloud ten times with each study period. Pronounce the *s* as *z* DO NOT *say* the letter *k*. Give ONLY the *sound* of *k*.
Note: Some methods used in this book are not traditional, but the author's own, developed around the particular needs of her students.

az k, az k, az k, az k, az k, az k, az k az k,
az k, az k, az k, az k, az k, az k, az k az k,

Repeat the following aloud ten times with each study period exaggerating the italicized words. The pronounciation is in parenthesis following the word.

1. You should *ask* (azk) to be admitted.
2. Why did you *ask* (azk) him?
3. *Ask* (azk) permission before coming.
4. Will she *ask* (azk) for a vacation?
5. Why not *ask* (azk) her?

When an action word ends in a whispered sound and the post tense is formed by adding *ed,* the *ed* is pronounced like *t.* Since *K* is a whispered sound, the past tense of ask (azk), asked is pronounced with a *t* sound: *asked* (azkt).

Memorize the following. Practice slowly at first so as not to give the *x* sound.

1. She *asked* (azkt) to be excused.
2. He *asked* (azkt) him to return before dark.
3. He had *asked* (azkt) to be admitted.
4. We *asked* (azkt) for advice.
5. She *asked* (azkt) the price of the book.

OTHER VERBS ENDING IN K

1. His friendly smile *masked* (maskt) his intentions of murder.

2. The dessert called *baked* (bakt) Alaska consisted of ice cream and cake.

3. The horse *balked* (bokt) at the railroad track.

4. The boat was watertight because he had *caulked* (kokt) it well.

5. It *irked* (urkt) him to wait.

6. She *worked* (wurkt) many hours to accomplish her goal.

7. We *marked* (markt) passages to be memorized.

8. She had *kinked* (kingt) her hair in an Afro style.

9. The engine of his car had *knocked* (nokt) badly for days.

10. The crowd *packed* (pakt) the ball park.

THE SOUND OF S

S is a whispered sound. Place the sides of the tongue against the upper jaw teeth with the sides curved upward, and place the tip of the tongue against the lower gums below the lower teeth. Now expel the breath in a soft sound *against the cutting edge of the lower teeth.* When a verb ends with the sound of *s* and must form its past tense by adding *ed,* the *ed* is pronounced like *t.*

Repeat the following aloud ten times with each study period, emphasizing the italicized words.

1. They were *blessed* (blest) with a baby girl. Note: the *noun* "blessed" is pronounced with two syllables.

2. He *passed* (past) the year studying very hard for his degree.

3. He *bypassed* (BI past) the dean and took his problem to the president.

4. The bread was *passed* (past) before grace was said.

5. She *passed* (past) an enjoyable evening with her friends.

6. He became tired of being *bossed* (bost) by his wife.
7. She *crossed* (krost) the street to avoid meeting him.
8. To show her sincerity, she *crossed* (krost) her heart.
9. He *grossed* (grost rhymes with *boast*) a million dollars last year.
10. She was punished because she *sassed* (sast) her mother.

THE WHISPERED P

P is a whispered sound. It is made by pressing the lips together, then forcing them apart with the breath without making a voiced sound. When a verb ending in *p* must form its past tense by adding *ed,* the *ed* is pronounced like *t.* Repeat the following aloud ten times with each study period, emphasizing the italicized words.

1. She *wrapped* (rapt) a scarf about her head.
2. He is *wrapped* (rapt) up in his work.
3. The gang *rapped* (rapt) until one o'clock in the morning.
5. He *helped* (hellpt) her into the car. (Be sure to sound the *l* in help.)
6. She had *helped* (hellpt) him with all his work.
7. The crowd was *whipped* (whipt) into a frenzy by this morning.
8. The man was *stripped* (stript) of all his property.
9. He *stopped* (stopt) at the best hotel in town.
10. She *dropped* (dropt) in for a visit.

THE WHISPERED F

F is a whispered sound. It is formed by placing the lower lip against the upper teeth, and forcing the breath quickly through the space between the teeth and lip. Since *f* is a whispered sound the *ed* following it in the past tense of the verb must be pronounced like *t.* Drill on the following exercise.

1. He *laughed* (laft) at his own mistakes.
2. Fools have *laughed* (laft) at geniuses.
3. The boys really *roughed* (ruft) it on their fishing trip.
4. When he became a success he *sloughed* (sluft) off his old friends.
5. The police dog *sniffed* (snift) out the hidden drugs.
6. She *stuffed* (stuft) the turkey with seasoned bread crumbs.
7. She *goofed* (gooft) up one opportunity after another.
8. They *goofed* (gooft) around when they should have been working.
9. The floor should be *buffed* (buft) every week.
10. He *coughed* (koft) a week before consulting a doctor.

THE SOUND OF SH

Sh is a whispered sound. To produce it place the tip of the tongue against the lower gums below the lower teeth, and press the sides of the tongue against the upper teeth. Expel the whispered breath through slightly protruding lips. Since *sh* is a whispered sound, the *ed* following it at the end of a verb is pronounced like *t.*

Repeat the following aloud ten times with each study period, emphasizing the italicized words.

1. Tears *rushed* (rusht) to her eyes.
2. The impatient river *rushed* (rusht) headlong to the sea.
3. Her dress was *splashed* (splasht) with ink.
4. Her dream would come true if she *wished* (wisht) upon a star.

5. The driving rain *washed* (washt) the car clean.

6. He *pushed* (poosht, oo as in book) himself hard to succeed.

7. He *fished* (fisht) around for an answer.

8. An economic depression resulted when the stock market *crashed* (krasht).

9. The small businessman is in danger of being *crushed* (krusht).

THE SOUND OF CH

The *ch* sound is a whispered sound. To make it, press the tip of the tongue firmly against the upper gum ridge with the sides pressed firmly against the upper teeth. Build up a column of air under pressure, then release the breath suddenly without using the voice. Since *ch* is a whispered sound, the *ed* following it at the end of a verb to form the past tense is pronounced like *t.*

Repeat the following aloud ten times with each study period, emphasizing the italicized words.

1. The old road *branched* (brancht) off toward the river.

2. His books have *reached* (reecht) millions.

3. She *reached* (reecht) out her hands in greeting.

4. He cannot be *reached* (reecht) at the hotel.

5. He *botched* (bocht) the job badly.

6. He *beached* (beecht) his boat on a sand bar.

7. He *clinched* (klincht) the argument with his last rebuttal.

8. The player was *benched* (bencht) for the remainder of the season.

9. She *latched* (lacht) the door before leaving.

10. He *notched* (nocht) a stick each time he won a game.

WHEN ED IS PRONOUNCED D

When *ed* represents the past tense or past participle of a verb, without forming an extra syllable, it is pronounced *d* when the preceding sound is a *voiced* sound. Study the following sentences.

1. He *begged* (begd) her to forgive him.
2. The sunlight *bathed* (baathd) the trees in a golden glow.
3. He *cared* (kard) more for his pets than he did for his friends.
4. He had *charged* (charjd, a as in father) too much for a used car.
5. He *pulled* (poold, oo as in book) the sled to the top of the hill.
6. She was *robbed* (robd) of her inheritance.
7. They *rubbed* (rubd) sticks together to make a fire.
8. He *lived* (livd) across the river.

16.

FAULTY SPEECH—V

1. *Do not say:* I *run* a mile yesterday.
   Say instead: I *ran* a mile yesterday.
2. *Do not say:* I *have* ran for president.
   Say instead: I *have run* for president.
3. *Do not Say:* I *sung* in the choir Sunday.
   Say instead: I *sang* in the choir Sunday.
4. *Do not say:* I *have sang* all my life.
   Say instead: I *have sung* all my life.
5. *Do not say: Have* you *spoke* to him about it?
   Say instead: Have you *spoken* to him about it?
6. *Do not say:* Who *done* it?
   Say instead: Who *did* it? Who *has done it?*

7. *Do not say:* I *have did* my lessons.
   Say instead: I *have done* my lessons.
8. *Do not say:* He *drawed* a rabbit in his book.
   Say instead: He *drew* a rabbit in his book.
9. *Do not say:* He *drunk* all the lemonade.
   Say instead: He *drank* all the lemonade.
10. *Do not say: Has* he *rang* the bell?
    Say instead: Has he *rung* the bell?
11. *Do not say:* She *hasn't wrote* me this week.
    Say instead: She *hasn't written* me this week.
12. *Do not say:* He *holped* him with his work.
    Say instead: She *helped* (hellpt) him with his work.

Note: "Holped" is not a word in the English language.

17.

FAULTY SPEECH—VI

Repeat the CORRECT expressions ten times with each practice period, putting more stress on the italicized words.

1. *Do not say:* The baby hasn't *fell* yet.
   Say instead: The baby hasn't *fallen* yet.
2. *Do not say:* Have you *froze* your hands?
   Say instead: Have you *frozen* your hands?
3. *Do not say* I *seen* him yesterday.
   Say instead: I *saw* him yesterday.
4. *Do not say:* I *haven't saw* him today.
   Say instead: I *haven't seen* him today.
5. *Do not say: Ain't* you gone yet?
   Say instead: Haven't you gone yet?
6. *Do not say:* I am smart, *ain't I?*
   Say instead: I am smart, *am I not?*
7. *Do not say:* I am smart, *aren't I?*
   Say instead: I am smart, *am I not?*

8. *Do not say:* He's handsome, *ain't he?*
   Say instead: He's handsome, *isn't he?*
9. *Do not say:* You are going, *ain't you?*
   Say instead: You are going, *aren't you?*
10. *Do not say:* I'll walk a little *ways* with you.
    Say instead: I'll walk a little *way* with you.
11. *Do not say:* She's *going on* forty.
    Say instead: She's *approaching* forty. She's *almost* forty.
12. *Do not say:* *Has* the paper *came* yet?
    Say instead: *Has* the paper *come* yet?

18.

IF, WITH WAS AND WERE

Many people are uncertain about the use of *was* and *were* with if. You can quickly learn when to use *was* and when to use *were* by learning a simple rule. When *if* is followed by a singular subject, use *was* when you are expressing a *fact.* In this case *if* means *since.* To test it out, try substituting the word *since* for *if* in the following sentences.

1. *If she was* there, why didn't she answer? (She was there.)

2. *If he was* there, why didn't he call? (He *was* there.)

3. *If she was* poor, she could get a scholarship. (She *was* poor.)

4. *If she was* annoyed, why didn't she leave? (She *was* annoyed.)

5. *If he was* her son, why didn't she claim him? (He *was* her son.)

6. *If it was* storming, you should have taken a cab. (It *was* storming.)

7. *If she was* ill, she should have called a doctor. (She *was* ill.)

8. *If it was* raining, she should have stayed at home. (It *was* raining.)

When *if* is followed by a singular subject, use *were* when you are expressing a condition *contrary to fact. If* in this case means supposing. You could substitute *suppose* for *if.* Remember, we are only talking of SINGULAR subjects. With plural subjects we always use *were,* regardless of the meaning. Repeat the following aloud ten times, emphasizing the italicized words.

1. *If I were* you, I wouldn't care. (*I am not* you.)
2. *If he were* here, he would wash the car. (He is *not* here.)
3. *If he were* trained, he would handle the job. (He is *not* trained.)
4. *If John were* here, it wouldn't have happened. (John is *not* here.)
5. If she were my child, I would punish her. (She is *not* my child.)
6. *If I were* hungry, I would eat. (I am *not* hungry.)
7. *If she were* wise, she would get married. (She is *not* wise.)
8. *If* the *farmer were* trained, he would make a profit. (The farmer is *not* trained.)
9. *If* the *river were* deep, we would use the boat. (The river is *not* deep.)
10. *If* the *climate were* warm, I wouldn't need a fur coat. (The climate is *not* warm.)

Note: With a plural subject we always use *were.* Examples:

1. *If they were lazy,* they could not make outstanding grades. (They are *not* lazy.)

2. *If they were* angry, why didn't they say no? (They *were* angry.)

In expressing concession, probability, regret or a wish always use *were.*

1. She looks *as if she were* fainting.
2. The tree looks *as if it were* dying.
3. I *wish* that *he were* here.
4. He *wishes* that *he were* president.
5. She *wishes* that *she were* somewhere else.

19.

FAULTY SPEECH—VII

Repeat the CORRECT expression ten times with each practice period, putting more stress on the italicized words.

1. *Do not say:* The storm *has blowed* the house down.
   Say instead: The storm *has blown* the house down.
2. *Do not say:* She *begin* to see her mistakes.
   Say instead: She *began* to see her mistakes.
3. *Do not say:* Her heart *has been broke* twice.
   Say instead: Her heart *has been broken* twice.
4. *Do not say:* He *has growed* larger.
   Say instead: He *has grown* larger.
5. *Do not say:* I *swum* a mile yesterday.
   Say instead: I *swam* a mile yesterday.
6. *Do not say:* He *had dove* into the lake.
   Say instead: He *had dived* into the lake.
7. *Do not say:* Have you *drank* your milk?
   Say instead: Have you *drunk* your milk?
8. *Do not say:* The chicken *has flew* the coop.
   Say instead: The chicken *has flown* the coop.

9. *Do not say: Have* you *ate* yet?
   Say instead: Have you *eaten* yet?
10. *Do not say:* He *et* his dinner early.
    Say instead: He *ate* his dinner early.
11. *Do not say:* She *has swam* every summer.
    Say instead: She *has swum* every summer.
12. *Do not say:* The balloons were *busting* all over.
    Say instead: The balloons were *bursting* all over.
13. *Do not say:* The wind *blowed* hard.
    Say instead: The wind *blew* hard.
14. *Do not say:* He *had drank* the coke.
    Say instead: He *had drunk* the coke.
15. *Do not say:* He *drunk* the coke.
    Say instead: He *drank* the coke.
16. *Do not say:* The boys *drug* the boat to shore.
    Say instead: The boys *dragged* the boat to shore.
17. *Do not say:* The car *has been stole.*
    Say instead: The car *has been stolen.*
18. *Do not say: Has* anyone *saw* the paper?
    Say instead: Has anyone *seen* the paper?
19. *Do not say:* I should *have brung* your book.
    Say instead: I should *have brought* your book.
20. *Do not say:* He *throwed* rocks into the river.
    Say instead: He *threw rocks* into the river.

20.

EACH OTHER AND ONE ANOTHER

Each other should be used in referring to two persons or two things; *one another* always refers to more than two. Drill on the following expressions until this fact is firmly fixed in your mind.

1. The *two* girls helped *each other* with their work.

2. The *two* men contradicted *each other* on the witness stand.

3. What the *two* women said conflicted with *each other's* statements.

4. The *two* sisters competed against *each other.*

5. The *two* top students challenged *each other* for first place.

6. The *two* contestants worked against *each other* for first place.

7. The *two* prize fighters fought *each other* for the championship.

8. *John* and *James* struggled with *each other* on the floor.

9. They were hard put to keep *Joe* and *Bill* from fighting *each other.*

10. The *United States* and *Canada* are friendly toward *each other.*

When referring to more than two, use *one another.*

1. The *group* of girls helped *one another* with their work.

2. *All* the men contradicted *one another* on the witness stand.

3. What the *four* women said conflicted with *one another's* statements.

4. *All* the sisters competed with *one another.*

5. *Students* in the top ten percent challenged *one another* for first place.

6. *All* the contestants worked against *one another* for first prize.

7. In a tournament the prize *fighters* fought *one another* for the championship.

8. A *gang* of boys struggled with *one another* on the floor.

9. They were hard put to keep the *group* of boys from fighting *one another.*

10. *Most* of the nations in the United Nations are friendly toward *one another.*

21.

SOME TROUBLESOME VERBS

SIT—SET

The verb *sit* is frequently confused with the verb *set.* You will have no difficulty with the two if you will learn the meaning and the principal parts of each. *Sit* means to assume a certain position, to be in a certain position, or to be in a certain place. Some persons think that lifeless things or lifeless objects cannot *sit,* but this idea is wrong. A lamp *sits* on a table, a chair *sits* on a porch, just as a person *sits* in a chair. If they are already there (in a certain place) when you observe them, they are *sitting.*

Learn the principal parts of the verb *sit* by memorizing the following statements. Emphasize the italicized words.

1. Today I *sit* alone. I am *sitting* alone. (present time).
2. Yesterday I *sat* alone. (past time).
3. I *have sat* alone many times before. (completed time).
4. Today the lamp *sits* on the table. The lamp *is sitting* on the table. (present time).
5. Yesterday the lamp *sat* on the table. (past time).
6. The lamp *has sat* on the table three days. (completed time).

SET

The verb *set* means to PUT something or someone in a pacticular place or to PLACE something or someone in a particular position or posture. Learn how to use *set* by drilling on the following statements, always emphasizing the italicized words. Remember, *set* means to *put* or *place* something or someone somewhere. All three forms of the principal parts of *set* are alike.

.1. Today he *set* the lamp on the table. (present time).

2. He is *setting* the lamp on the table. (present time).

3. Yesterday he *set* the lamp on the table. (past time).

4. He *has set* the lamp there many times. (completed time).

5. The mother *set* the baby on the floor. (present time).

6. She *is setting* the baby on the floor. (present time).

7. Yesterday she *set* the baby on the floor. (past time).

8. She *has* set the baby on the floor many times before. (completed time).

LIE—LAY

The verb *lie* is often confused with the verb *lay.* You will have no difficulty with the two if you will learn the meaning and the principal parts of each. *Lie* means to assume a position or place. Some people think that the verb *lie* can be used only when speaking of living persons or things, but this is not true. A hat *lies* on the ground, a scarf *lies* on the porch, just as a person *lies* on a bed.

Learn the principal parts of this verb by drilling on the following statements, emphasizing the italicized words.

1. Today I *lie* down. (present time).
2. Today I *am lying* down. (present time).
3. Yesterday I *lay* down. (past time).

4. I *have lain* down many times. (completed time).
5. The dog *lies* at my feet. (present time).
6. The dog *lay* there all day. (past time).
7. They found his bone *lying* in the yard. (not laying).

LAY

The verb *lay* means to PUT or PLACE something or someone in a horizontal position or a position of rest. You can substitute *place* or *put* for *lay.* But *place or put cannot be substituted for lie.* Learn when to use *lay* by memorizing the following statements. Repeat the statements aloud ten times while emphasizing the italicized words.

1. Today I *lay* the book on my desk. (present time).
2. I *am laying* the book on my desk. (present time).
3. Yesterday I *laid* the book on my desk. (past time).
4. I *was laying* the book on my desk. (past time).
5. I *have laid* it there before. (completed time).
6. She *had laid* the hat on the table. (completed time).

22.

WORDS ENDING IN SELF

Words ending in *self* may be used in only three ways: (1) after a verb to refer to the subject; (2) after a preposition to refer to the subject; (3) used beside a noun or a pronoun for emphasis.

AFTER A VERB TO REFER TO THE SUBJECT

1. I *taught myself* to play the piano.
2. We *controlled ourselves* and ate very little.
3. She *supports herself* by working very hard.

4. She *gave herself* a vacation.
5. After a rest she will *be herself* again.
6. *Ask yourself* why you didn't win
8. She *worked herself* into a state of exhaustion.
9. He failed because he *doubted himself.*
10. I *gave myself* a facial with fragrant cream.

AFTER A PREPOSITION TO REFER TO THE SUBJECT

1. He gave her a picture *of himself.*
2. He referred *to himself.*
3. John wrote a letter *to himself.*
4. I shall save the food *for myself.*
5. She wrote the article *by herself.*
6. We are keeping the secret *between ourselves.*
7. You should try the dress *on yourself.*
8. The authors shared the research *among themselves.*

BESIDE A NOUN OR A PRONOUN FOR EMPHASIS

1. *John himself* is the one who did it.
2. *I myself* went with him.
3. *She herself* wrote the article.
4. *We ourselves* are to blame.
5. *You yourself* asked that it be done.
6. *We ourselves* would never do such a thing.
7. The *authors themselves* would never submit to intimidation.
8. The *horse itself* opened the gate.

Note: Myself may be used as a substitute for *me,* but is frowned on by most grammarians. It is considered substandard to use the objective forms of the pronoun as substitutes for any word ending in *self.*

23.

FAULTY SPEECH—VIII

1. *Do not say: myself* and *wife* went to the show.
   Say instead: My *wife* and *I* went to the show.
2. *Do not say:* She wanted *Mary* and *myself* to go.
   Say instead: She wanted *Mary* and *me* to go.
3. *Do not say:* He gave it to *myself.*
   Say instead: He gave it *to me.*
4. *Do not say:* My *wife* and *myself* went yesterday.
   Say instead: My *wife* and *I* went yesterday.
5. *Do not say: Mr. Smith* and *myself* will visit you.
   Say instead: Mr. Smith and *I* will visit you.
6. *Do not say:* He greeted *my daughter* and *myself.*
   Say instead: He greeted *my daughter* and *me.*

24.

REVIEW OF NOUNS AND PRONOUNS

Nouns are words that stand for people or things, such as, *John, books,* and *house.* Pronouns are words that stand for nouns, such as *he, it* and *they.* A simple rule concerning nouns is: All nouns are either acting as the subject of a sentence, or they are the object of a sentence. When a noun is the person or thing doing something it is called the *subject.* When a noun is the person or thing to which something is done it is called the *object.*

Since pronouns are words that stand for nouns, the same rule applies to pronouns. The *subjective* form of a pronoun is used as a subject. The subjective forms are: *I, you, he, she, it, we,* and *they.* Examples:

1. *I* am going home.
2. *You* will find it there.

3. *He* is a good boy.
4. *She* tried very hard.
6. *We* will be late.
7. *They* came yesterday.

PRONOUNS USED AS OBJECTS OF PREPOSITIONS

Pronouns with prepositions will be considered separately because of the difficulty they present to a majority of persons. A *preposition* is a word (other than a verb) *placed before* its object, either a noun or a pronoun. Pronouns must change their forms when used as objects. (Note: The pronouns *you* and *it* are exceptions. They do not change forms when used as objects.)

The *objective* forms of the pronoun should always be used as the object of a preposition. The objective forms of the pronoun are: *me, you, him, her, it, us, them,* and *whom.* The most commonly used prepositions are: *between, against, after, before, except, like, to, with, of, in, on, by,* and *since.*

Drill on the following statements, emphasizing the italicized words. Use the sentences as models and start your own private collection.

1. The secret was *between him* and *her.*
2. Let this remain *between you* and *me.*
3. Just *between you* and *me,* I don't care.
4. You should have gone *with Mary* and *me.*
5. All the families *but them* agreed to the project.
6. Everyone came *except them.*
7. What does she have *against you* and *me?*
8. Don't try to behave *like us;* be yourselves.
9. Everybody is going *but us.*
10. We shall select a gift *for him* and *her.*

11. He came *after me* in the line.
12. She arrived *before us,* and left *before him.*
13. How could the city people eat *without us* farmers.
14. We farmers must *feed them* and *us.* (verb)
15. This must be settled *between them* and *us.*
16. Did you invite all the girls *except her?*
17. Everyone *but Julie* and *her* is working today.
18. *Between you* and *me,* don't ever forget.

Note: Never, never say: "This is between you and I." say instead: "This is between you and me."

25.

BUILD YOUR OWN VOCABULARY

You don't really have to remember the rules, or to know about subjects, objects and prepositions in order to speak well. If you will memorize commonly used expressions where these forms are used, you can forget about the rules. This small book cannot, of course, include all of the ready-to-use expressions you will need. But you can use this book as a guide and work out the expressions you are in need of, using the ones in the book as models. To develop a large working vocabulary, use small notebooks (3 x 5 inches) in which to record short statements and phrases. You will find that a small notebook is the quickest way to develop your vocabulary, because you may take it with you wherever you go and study in spare moments when you are not busy.

26.

DO NOT ADD LETTERS OR SOUNDS

THE ADDITION OF S

Perhaps the most substandard speech habit (aside from the misuse of *have* and *has*) is the addition of extra letters and sounds. The most common is the addition of *s* to such words as men, women, and children. This speech fault will brand anyone as an illiterate. If you have developed this habit, start now to correct it. Memorize the following expressions, and exaggerate the *n* sound when practicing.

N is a voiced sound. It is made by pressing the tongue against the upper gum ridge, and the sides of the tongue against the upper jaw teeth to block the air passage at the sides. Expel the breath through the nose while making a humming sound.

The pronunciation is in parenthesis following the word.

1. All *children* (CHIL dren) need clothes and shoes.. (not chilluns or childrens)

2. The *children* (CHIL dren) came early to lunch. (not chilluns)

3. *Men* are usually thoughtful. (not mens)

4. We'll have to wait for the *men* to return. (not mens)

5. Most *women* (WIM in) have happy temperaments. (not womens)

6. The *people* (PEE pl) will elect their candidate (not peoples)

7. *Women* (WIM in) who enjoy motherhood make good mothers. (not womens)

8. The *people* (PEE pl) of this country are generally united. (not peoples)

ADDING EXTRA SOUNDS

Some of the most careful speakers mispronounce the following words by adding extra sounds. You should strive to correct this bad speech habit. Drill daily on these words until you have mastered them.

Note: in the pronunciation key in parenthesis, double letters are used to indicate a long vowel, or to emphasize the sound of a consonant. The syllable to be stressed is capitalized.

1. Athlete (ATH leet). Don't say (ATH a leet).
2. athletic (ath LET ik). Don't say (ath a LET ik).
3. Burglar (BUR gler). Don't say (BUR ga ler).
4. pamphlet (PAM flit). Don't say PAM fa lit).
5. translate (TRANS laat). Don't say (TRANS a laat).
6. chimney (CHIM nee). Don't say (CHIM a nee, or CHIM blee).
7. lightning (LIIT ning). Dont say (LII te ning).
8. umbrella (um BREL a). Don't say (um ba REL a).
9. electoral (e LEK ter al). Dont' say (e lek TOR ee al).
10. grievous (GREE ves). Don't say (GREE vee us).
11. miscievous (MIS chi ves). Don't say (mis CHEE vee us).
12. elm (ellm). One syllable *only.* Bring out the *l* but don't say (EL em).

Drill on the following sentences until the correct pronunciation is thoroughly etched on your mind. Exaggerate the italicized words while practicing.

1. The *athlete* sprained an ankle.
2. The *athletic* event was held yesterday.
3. *Burglars* broke into the building.
4. He distributed the *pamphlets* to the customers.
5. He helped to *translate* the book into English.
6. The *chimney* was made of fieldstone.
7. *Lightning* struck the old house.

8. The *umbrella* was bent by the wind.
9. All the *electoral* votes were counted.
10. He made a *grievous* mistake.
11. He was a *mischievous* boy.
12. The old *elm* swayed in the breeze.
13. We shall have the *film* developed.

27.

DO NOT PRONOUNCE SILENT LETTERS

Many English words have letters that must not be pronounced. These letters are colled consonants. Consonants are all letters of the alphabet other than *a, e, i, o, u,* and *y.* These letters are called vowels. The letters that must not be pronounced are called "silent" consonants. Some of the most important words that have silent consonants are listed below. Drill on the spelling and pronunciation until you have mastered both.

lamb (lam)
climb (kliim)
comb (kom)
crumb (krum)
doubt (dout)
subtle (SUT el)
limb (lim)
thumb (thum)
gnat (nat)
sign (siin)
handkerchief (HANG ker chif)
sigh (sii)
corps (kor, like apple core)
walk (wawk, rhymes with hawk)
talk (tawk)
calm (kawm)
palm (pawn)
psalm (sawm)
drought (drout)
debt (det)
often (OF en)
glisten (GLIS en)
mortgage (MOR gij)
schism (SIZ em)
soften (SOF en)
vehicle (VEE i kel)
listen (LIS en)
handsome (HAN sem)
autumn (AW tem)
island (II lend)

Note: In the pronunciation key in parenthesis, double letters indicate a long vowel. The syllable to be stressed is capitalized. The *t* is pronounced in *soft* but silent in *soften.*

Repeat the following aloud ten times with each practice period, stressing the italicized words.

1. I shall *comb* my hair.
2. A *subtle* smile betrayed his real feelings.
3. He *doubted* her sincerity.
4. I shall *walk* alone in the *calm* of the evening.
5. The *palm* trees were damaged by the *drought.*
6. The dew *glistens* on the *autumn* leaves.
7. He is *often* in *debt* but the mortgage is paid.
8. The Peace *Corps* (kor) workers were dedicated men.
9. A *corps* of policemen surrounded the area.
10. The band *corps* practiced all week.
11. The U.S. Marine *Corps* performed for the president.
12. A *corps* of engineers drew the blueprint for the expressway.

28.

WORDS THAT DO NOT EXIST IN STANDARD USAGE

Careless speakers sometimes use words that do not exist. The most common are: *disremember, irregardless, disregardless, ways,* (as a substitute for way), and *hope* or *holp,* (as past tense for help). *Ways* should be used only as a plural for *way.* It should never be used as a substitute for *way* or to mean distance. Only an illiterate would use *holp* to mean help.

1. *Do not say:* I *disremember* where I put it.
   Say instead: I *forgot* where I put it.

2. *Do not say: Disregardless* of what he said, I still don't believe it.
   Say instead: Regardless of what he said, I still don't believe it.
4. *Do not say: Irregardless* of the price, I shall buy it.
   Say instead: Regardless of the price, I shall buy it.
5. *Do not say:* It's a long *ways* from here.
   Say instead: It's a long *way* from here.
6. *Do not say:* You have come a long *ways.*
   Say instead: You have come a long *way.*
7. *Do not say:* I *bees* hungry.
   Say instead: I *am* hungry.

WAYS, AS A PLURAL OF WAY

Ways used as a plural of way, should mean, "method, plan, or manner."

1. She has many strange *ways.*
2. The plan is defective in many *ways.*
3. She didn't like his *ways.*

29.

CAN AND MAY

Can is a word meaning *to have the ability* or *power,* or *to be able* to do something. *May* means to have *permission,* or the *possibility.* For many years educators have debated on the use of these two words. Today the distincition is disappearing, and the two are often used interchangeably. But to be correct, you must make a distinction between them. Study the following. The statements are correct.

1. He *can* solve the problem easily.
2. She *can* play baseball as well as he.

3. The child *can* talk without a lisp.
4. She *may* go to camp if she wishes.
5. The author *may* change the wording in the script.
6. *May* I borrow your pen?

30.

FEWER AND LESS

Fewer and *less* are often used interchangeably, but to be completely correct you must make a distinction between the two. *Less* means to a smaller amount or degree. *Fewer* means a smaller number. Study carefully the sentences below.

1. This version of the Bible is *less* popular than the other.
2. This cake requires *less* sugar.
3. The dress required *less* material to make.
4. The job is *less* than perfect.
5. Let's have *less* talk and more action.

1. *Fewer* people came than anticipated.
2. *Fewer* trains are running today than ten years ago.
3. There are *fewer* apples to the bushel than peaches.
4. Today, parents are desiring *fewer* children in the family.
5. Let's have *fewer* words and more action.

31.

CONFUSION ABOUT SHALL AND WILL

Even though the rules governing the use of *shall* and *will* are growing weaker, and more and more people are using will in both places, careful speakers are careful to make the distinction between the two. Let us review some simple rules governing the two.

To express FUTURE TIME USE SHALL with *I* and *we,* but WILL with *you, he, she, it,* and *they.* Study carefully the following sentences.

1. After I graduate, *I shall* move to another state.
2. After we pay the mortgage, *we shall* celebrate.
3. When I go home, *I shall* telephone him.
4. *We shall* leave tomorrow.

1. After he graduates, *he will* move to another state.
2. After they pay the mortgage, *they will* celebrate.
3. When she goes home, *she will* telephone him.
4. When you have completed the job, *you will* be happy.
5. When the clock strikes twelve, *it will* be too late.

When the speaker expresses DETERMINATION, a COMMAND, or a PROMISE use WILL with *I* and *we,* but SHALL with *you, he, she, it,* and *they.* The confusion is created by the fact that the rules are reversed in expressing determination or a command.

1. *I will* go whether you like it or not.
2. *We will* go whether you like it or not.
3. *I will* punish you if you disobey.
4. *We will* apply the rules against violators.
5. *I will* meet you there, I promise you.
6. *We will* have good government, in spite of the conflicts.

1. *You shall* do what your father demands.
2. *You shall* pay the mortgage or we will forclose.
3. *He shall* do as I say.
4. *She shall* go despite her crying.
5. *It shall* become the rule despite their disapproval.
6. *They shall* remain regardless of their feelings.

32.

COMPARING PERSONS AND THINGS

Some people make mistakes in comparing two or more things. This type of error can be serious. When we tell the difference between two things, or among three or more things we are said to be comparing them. When we are comparing *two* things or *two* persons we usually add *er* to the word used to describe. Example: *tall, taller.* Mary is *tall,* but Sue is *taller.* But with some descriptive words we do not add *er* to compare two things. Instead we use *more* before the descriptive word. Example: *beautiful, more beautiful.* Mary is *beautiful,* but Sue is *more beautiful.* One thing that you must always remember: *Never use MORE if the description word ends in er.* To say, "This is *more better* than that" is an unforgivable sin.

COMPARING TWO

Repeat aloud with each study period and stress the italicized words.

1. Helen is *prettier* than Mary.
2. It is *cooler* in the spring than in the summer.
3. Mr. Smith is *wiser* than Mr. Brown.
4. John is *braver* than James.
5. Longfellow is a *greater* poet than Edgar Guest.
6. Steel is *stronger* than iron.
7. Roses smell *sweeter* than violets.
8. John works *harder* than Mary.
9. A bus is *more convenient* than a trolley.
10. Blue is a *more beautiful* color than green.
11. Bobby is *worse behaved* than Joe.
12. Susie is *better behaved* than Sally.
13. The boy is *less friendly* than the girl.
14. Susie is *less worthy* to receive the award than Mary.

COMPARING MORE THAN TWO

In comparing *three* or *more* persons or things we usually add *est* to the descriptive word, or we use *most* before the descriptive word.

1. Helen is the *prettiest* of all the girls.
2. Spring is the *coolest* season of the four seasons.
3. Mr. Smith is the *wisest* man in town.
4. John is the *bravest* boy of them all.
5. Longfellow is one of the *greatest* American poets.
6. Steel is the *strongest* of all.
7. Roses smell the *sweetest* of all the flowers.
8. Jane works *hardest* of all the students.
9. An automobile is the *most convenient* means of transportation.
10. Red is the *most beautiful* of all the colors.
11. Jodie is the *worst behaved* child in the neighborhood.
12. Julie is the *best behaved* of all the girls.
13. John is *least friendly* of the three.
14. Dorothy is the *least worthy* of them all.

33.

FAULTY SPEECH—IX

1. *Do not say:* He is the *tallest* of the two.
   Say instead: He is the *taller* of the two.
2. *Do not say:* He is *more kinder* than his brother.
   Say instead: He is *kinder* than his brother.
3. *Do not say:* This book is *more lighter* than that one.
   Say instead: This book is *lighter* than that one.
4. *Do not say:* Poetry is *more easier* to learn than prose.
   Say instead: Poetry is *easier* to learn than *prose.*

5. *Do not say:* She should sing *more louder.*
   Say instead: She should sing *more loudly.* or *She* should sing *louder.*
6. *Do not say:* This is *more better* than that.
   Say instead: This is *better* than that.
7. *Do not say:* She works puzzles *more easier* than he.
   Say instead: She works puzzles *more easily* than he does.

34.
IT IS "I"

Many speakers sometime use the objective form of the pronoun that follows the verb *be.* This is considered *incorrect* by most grammarians and should never be used. The simple rule is this: *When any form of the verb BE is used as the main verb, the pronoun following it must be a subjective pronoun.* The forms of the verb *be* are: *am, is, are, was, were, being,* and *been.* The following sentences may appear awkward, but they are correct and you should memorize them all.

1. I *am she.*
2. It *is I.*
3. These *are they.*
4. This *is he.*
5. Those *were they.*
6. It might have *been he.*
7. Do you think it *was she?*
8. This *is she.*
9. That *is I.*
10. It must have *been we.*

Note: There is an exception to this rule: Many grammarians are agreeing that "This is me" is acceptable English.